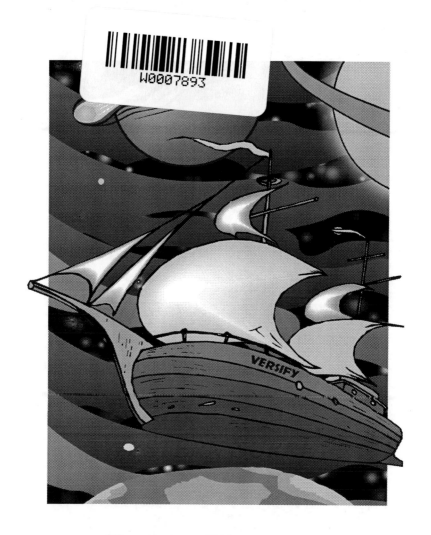

POETIC VOYAGES
WESTERN SURREY

Edited by Simon Harwin

First published in Great Britain in 2002 by
YOUNG WRITERS
Remus House,
Coltsfoot Drive,
Peterborough, PE2 9JX
Telephone (01733) 890066

HB ISBN 0 75433 432 5
SB ISBN 0 75433 433 3

FOREWORD

Young Writers was established in 1991 with the aim to promote creative writing in children, to make reading and writing poetry fun.

This year once again, proved to be a tremendous success with over 88,000 entries received nationwide.

The Poetic Voyages competition has shown us the high standard of work and effort that children are capable of today. It is a reflection of the teaching skills in schools, the enthusiasm and creativity they have injected into their pupils shines clearly within this anthology.

The task of selecting poems was therefore a difficult one but nevertheless, an enjoyable experience. We hope you are as pleased with the final selection in *Poetic Voyages Western Surrey* as we are.

CONTENTS

St Bartholomew's CE Primary School, Haslemere

The Poems

LOST PIE

I'm Indiana Slime.
I've got no time.
I'm looking for a pie.
Ahh! Look in the sky.
Monster birds attacking!
They keep on hacking.
But I zoom in my jeep,
Past the rock heap,
Up and down,
Round and round,
I've found the pie so I have to say
Bye.

Colby Falconer (8)
Edgeborough School

NIGHT DRIVE

We get in the car,
Off we set,
Down the road,
Miss a cat,
Round and round,
See a fox,
Turn the corner,
Get back home,
Sit down and watch TV!

Oliver Keene (8)
Edgeborough School

WATERSKIING

Ready, get set, go!
Make sure you don't fall over the waves.
Jumping, spinning, twisting.
Oh dear we are getting near rocks,
Turn around,
There is the finish line,
We *won!*

Charlie Metcalf (8)
Edgeborough School

THE CHEETAH WHO GOT TRICKED

Slowly prowling through the grass,
What do I see?
A young antelope slowly getting near.
Now is the time to pounce,
Here it comes,
Oh no it's a fast one.
Got it.
Boy it's heavy,
I will drag it under a tree.
Hey come back!
There goes my tea.

James Mitchell (8)
Edgeborough School

THE SKI RACE

Over the jumps,
Doing tricks,
Trying to miss every stick.
Round the corners,
Down the cliff,
Grinding to the nearest lift.
Watch the ice
It's very fast,
If you fall over
You'll come last.

Jack Richards (8)
Edgeborough School

THE RACE

The big red engine racing around the track
At every corner I hear the loud crack,
Of Ferrari racing cars flying through the air
Scaring people who fall off their chair.
What an exciting race it's going to be
As the cars skid through the tunnel you can see
Bright yellow sparks shining, spitting from the tyres
And oh no, help, the engine may catch fire.
What a surprise five laps left,
Who will be the winner? What a finish!
What a race!
I'll be back to this exciting place.

Jamie Ferguson (8)
Edgeborough School

A CARRIER PIGEON

I'm a carrier pigeon flying high,
Flap, flap I rise to the sky.
I have a message,
A message from a friend
A message to give at my journey's end.
I'm a carrier pigeon from over the sea
Look at me flying so low, whoopee!

Charlie Martin (7)
Edgeborough School

TIME MACHINE

In we go,
Back, back, back.
Back to Rome and then the Celts.
Forwards a bit,
If it breaks down
You're stuck!

Ben Kerawala (8)
Edgeborough School

My Visit On The London Eye

I'm going on the London Eye,
Going round and round in circles,
It goes round very slowly now,
And I feel very lonely.

I want my mum and dad to come,
But they're still having coffee,
I want to jump out now and,
Find myself eating toffee.

James Roberts (8)
Edgeborough School

THE FLAPCOO

The Flapcoo is a creature that lives upon the swamps.
If anything comes near it, it shrieks and howls and stomps.
It has golden feathers that give it away so it hides among the green,
And as you might have guessed already, it is never ever seen.
It may look like a bird, but that is not the right word,
For it has gills just like a fish,
And if you hear it you may wish to see the Flapcoo.
It lives on a diet of worms and bugs,
And takes a sip out of abandoned mugs.
It has a sharp beak topped with an iron fist,
The only problem with the Flapcoo is that it doesn't exist.

Matthew Knowles (9)
Edgeborough School

ELLA

Ella is our puppy,
She really is a laugh,
She chases my brothers round the house,
And chews my shoes in half.

She's black and gold with big black eyes,
And when my dad came in one night
She was his surprise.
She's very sweet with a capital S
And out of all dogs she's definitely the best.

Sometimes she is annoying, but often she is cool,
She's like a little sister and she loves her bouncing ball.
She has four big paws and a cold wet nose,
And on each big paw she has four big toes.

She only has little legs so she can't walk very far.
But she's really good when she goes in the car.
She's six months old and full of fun
And soon her training will be done.

I love her
And I hope she loves me.

She'll be a champion
Just wait, you'll see.

Katie Thomas (9)
Edgeborough School

LOVE

Love is bright pink,
The taste of a banana sweet.
It smells like a red rose.
It has the looks of a graceful swan.
Love sounds like the smooth tune of a harp,
Love is soft.

Alex Rossides (10)
Lanesborough Preparatory School

HAPPINESS

Happiness is the sweetest smell,
A smell of garden flowers,
Children playing hide-and-seek,
Passing happy hours.

Happiness is the brightest colour,
Scarlet, yellow and lime,
Fresh fruit salads good to eat,
Having wonderful times.

Happiness is peace in our world,
No more wars and fighting,
Countries living friends with all,
Problems solved by writing.

Chris Maclean (9)
Lanesborough Preparatory School

REMEMBRANCE

We'll remember the day and the hour.
We'll remember the deaths of the Great War.
We'll remember it, yes, we'll remember it.
We'll remember the poppies coming up creating a field of red.

Poppies grow, bodies lie, all in Flanders field.
Oh we'll remember the day, the minute, the hour.
Poppies come up and bodies fall. Oh, we'll remember it.
You and I will stand on the 11th day of the 11th month
For a minute, and remember you.

Harry Glasspool (9)
Lanesborough Preparatory School

BATTLE

The noise is deafening
As bullets take out my comrades.
All around me I hear
Their agonising screams.

We spend hours in cold wet trenches
Knee deep in mud, water and rats.
The air around us is filled with choking smoke
As mustard gas rolls towards us.

As another charge goes forwards
More people are brought down.
Soon it will be my turn to go over the top
And meet my comrades in Heaven.

Edward Thatcher (9)
Lanesborough Preparatory School

ANGER

Anger is red
It tastes bitter and sour
And smells like burning flesh
Anger looks like blood
Streaming out of a wound
It sounds like screaming
Anger feels like I'm lying on spikes!

James Simpson (9)
Lanesborough Preparatory School

I REMEMBER

I remember the soldiers who lost their lives
And couldn't go home to their waiting wives
I remember the soldiers who will never know
How it feels to watch their children grow
I remember the young men who lay down to die
In Flanders field so that you and I
Can live our lives in a world that is free
I remember all this when I wear my poppy.

Edward Longdon (10)
Lanesborough Preparatory School

WHEN I'M HAPPY

When I'm happy I feel like I'm up in the clouds
Talking to the stars with a happy feeling in my head.

When I'm happy everything's bright and cheerful.

When I'm happy it's as though I've just scored the winning goal
In the World Cup Final and everyone's cheering and shouting.

When I'm happy I feel like fresh hay and golden flowers.

When I'm happy I feel joyful and laughing.

Matthew Carey (9)
Lanesborough Preparatory School

REMEMBRANCE

S   oldiers fighting, killing and dying,
O   verhead bombers and fighters fly killing from the air,
L   ightning flashes as soldiers fight,
D   ying,
I   f only there was peace,
E   very day one thousand soldiers lie dead,
R   emember them to this day,
S   uch a waste!

Thomas Curtress (9)
Lanesborough Preparatory School

ANGER

Anger is sparkling red
It tastes of sour sweets
And smells like burning smoke
Anger looks like an exploding mind
It sounds like screaming
And is pain!

Tom Saville (9)
Lanesborough Preparatory School

POPPIES

P eace forgotten in the midst of Hell.
O verhead the rain comes down in balls of lead.
P utrid water, rat's blood and death, scuttling around.
P lanes come down in screaming balls of fire.
I ntense evil lurks behind failure.
E ternal sounds of guns and despair, cowering in the trenches.
S ome day, though, we will come out on top.

George Savage (10)
Lanesborough Preparatory School

HAPPINESS

When I am happy
I feel like I am sky blue
It tastes like root beer
Going down my throat.
It smells of primroses
In the sun.
If I listen I can hear
Puffins squawking
Merrily in the sun.
I feel like I'm in Heaven
That's what I call happiness.

Andrew Rice (10)
Lanesborough Preparatory School

CALM MOOD

When I'm calm,
I'm like a sea without waves
Like a bird gliding in the air,
When I'm calm,
I could lie in the sun under a palm tree.

Toby Cooper (9)
Lanesborough Preparatory School

IN FLANDERS FIELD

In Flanders field the floods are high
Puddles of blood drip through the mud
Brave men seek for freedom
Finding only the stench of death.

Tanks and planes bomb the cities
Forcing people to flee from death
Loyal troops defend their queen
And save Britain from its doom.

Robbie Marriott (10)
Lanesborough Preparatory School

HAPPINESS

Shades of orange come up in my head
A burst of taste through my mouth
The smell of roses come up my nose
My family and friends become one big photo in my head
The sound of my piano when I've practised so hard
I feel so happy inside.

William Davies (10)
Lanesborough Preparatory School

POPPY

P   ity the soldiers we sent off to war
O   ver to France to be slaughtered and maimed
P   oppies now sway on their lonely graves
P   eace takes the place of death and destruction
Y   et we will remember them forever and a day.

Jonathan Smith (9)
Lanesborough Preparatory School

POPPIES

Poppies, standing watching battle
Over fields bare of cattle.
Peace is gone and won't be back.
Please make the soldiers stop in their tracks
You must take the torch and hold it high
In remembrance of the soldiers who die.
England's soldier does his best
Soldiers of England shall never rest.

Henry Duncan (10)
Lanesborough Preparatory School

POPPY

P   roudly poppies grow in Flanders field.
O   ver the many fallen gruesome bodies.
P   eople lying in graves bullet-ridden and dead.
P   eace is what they fought for, not to be forgotten.
Y   ears pass, the poppy remains the symbol of war dead.

Ben Rusholme (10)
Lanesborough Preparatory School

SHELLS

S tepping over dead bodies in a muddy plain,
H earing wounded men cry with pain,
E very day the horrors of the trenches,
L ice, rats, mud, pouring rain drenches,
L ines of soldiers stumbling over no-man's-land,
S taggering towards the enemy bags of sand.

Andrew Tyler (10)
Lanesborough Preparatory School

THE GREAT FIRE OF LONDON

The baker went to put his bread,
In the oven which shined so red,
But he didn't know that in the night,
The whole town would be shining bright.

Before he got to eat his porridge,
The whole town would be shining orange,
He didn't know he would bellow,
When the town went up in yellow.

He didn't know a fire would spread,
Just from his tasty load of bread,
All the way from the square,
To wipe the town completely bare.

That the next day the news of the fire
Would be told by the town crier,
The news of so much death,
Caused by the fire's hot, smoky breath.

Just from a cause, so, so small,
A fire which would even get the town hall,
When the fire hit you'd have to run,
Just because of some overcooked bun.

Ross Vinten (9)
Lanesborough Preparatory School

RIVERS

Rivers here, rivers there
Rivers rushing everywhere
Bubbling, frothing and flowing away,
Whirlpools to waterfalls changing every day.

Flowing rivers shimmering in the sun
Ripples spreading, fading out of sight
Flowing around the world in all different forms
Transforming into all they like.

William Ayres (10)
Lanesborough Preparatory School

CLOCKS

A clock keeps time
A clock keeps rhythm,
The day and the date,
To great precision.

A clock can be big,
A clock can be small,
It can stand on the mantelpiece,
Or hang on the wall.

A clock can run from electricity,
A clock can run from a spring,
Sand and water
Can also make a clock ring.

A clock can be found anywhere.
At home, on a church and at school.
It can be made of wood, plastic or metal
A very useful tool.

Alexander Lake (10)
Lanesborough Preparatory School

THE HIDDEN MARSH

In the mist between the moors
There is a hidden marsh
With murky, bubbling water.
And a secret waterfall
Swirling and cascading
Onto moss-covered rocks.

Brooks and springs gurgle
Into the marsh.
Dappled light shines
Between the swaying trees
In the mist between the moors
There is a hidden marsh.

James Whittle (10)
Lanesborough Preparatory School

PEARL DIVING

Diving for pearls can be dangerous.
It can also be disappointing
You open up the biggest clam
And find nothing except a slimy black creature.

Diving for pearls can be fun
And if you're lucky you can get expensive pearls
You can sell them for lots of money
At the end of the day get rich.

Either way, whether you're lucky -
Or you're not, whether it's dangerous
Or it's fun, that is the way of life.

J Noy (10)
Lanesborough Preparatory School

HISS

Hiss is my snake
What does he do?
He hisses around
And looks for mice.

Where does he look?
In a mouse hole
The problem is
The cat gets there first.

Oliver Moger (9)
Lanesborough Preparatory School

ANTICIPATION

I'm looking forward to getting together with my family,
I'm looking forward to getting presents,
I'm looking forward to Christmas,
I'm looking forward to all the fun,
I'm looking forward to no school,
I'm looking forward to Christmas lunch,
I'm looking forward to my Advent calendar.

I like Christmas lunch,
I like Christmas pudding,
I like playing in the snow,
I like making snowmen,
I like decorating the tree,
I like all the sun,
I like all the presents,
I like all the excitement.

Guy Partridge (9)
Lanesborough Preparatory School

Time Flies By

Time flies by
I gobble down my breakfast.
Time flies by
I'm late for school.
    There's no time!

Time flies by
It's break time already.
Time flies by
It's the end of break!
    There's no time!

Time flies by
It's home time already.
Time flies by
Now I'm home.
    There's no time!

Time flies by
Now I can play.
Time flies by
'Bedtime' says Mum!

    There's no time!

James Turner (10)
Lanesborough Preparatory School

TIME

Time can be bad and time can be good for instance:
I don't have time to do my homework,
I don't have time to go to bed,
I don't have time to go to school.

These are the things I do have time for:
I have time to watch TV,
I have time to go on the PC,
I have time to eat sweets.

Sometimes time is horrible:
Weekends pass too quickly,
Holidays pass too quickly,
Your birthday passes too quickly,
Christmas passes too quickly,
And Easter passes too quickly.
Why do things pass so quickly?

Andrew Mulvany (9)
Lanesborough Preparatory School

FOOTBALL POEM

I walked onto a muddy pitch,
The opposition were strong,
They stood there in the roaring wind
In blue strips with red trim.

Their team were strong and very skilled
They immediately put pressure on us,
They put two past Darren our keeper
In about twenty-nine seconds.

The whistle suddenly blew for half-time,
We trudged in groaning oh blast,
Oh bang they really are truly great
We haven't got a chance.

We walked back on
Our hearts held in our mouths
No wonder why, they pounded us
Just as much as before.

We were really glad when it ended
'Never mind,' said Darren 'I'll talk to
Coach, we need more
Training because we lost thirty-six to five.'

William Peters (10)
Lanesborough Preparatory School

ALIENS

When aliens landed from outer space
They invaded my school for jelly
They came in with their splatters
Splat! Splat! Splat! Splat!

First Mrs Broom went down
And then Mr Kicety got shot
Until everybody was splattered
With icing sugar green.

Hamish Bigsmore came up to an alien
And said 'Take me to your leader'
'All right then, but only if you
Show me where the green jelly is.'

I saw this and knew I had to do something
So I got the nearby fire extinguisher
And came out and said
'Put your hands in the air.'

They shouted and screamed and ran away
The next day I went to school
All the girls liked me, they called me Wonder William
I was nominated best in the year.

Stefan Wichtowski
Lanesborough Preparatory School

THE PORTRAIT

In a house with no life and dust,
There is a portrait of Sir Richard Frust;
His nose is sharp and his face is long,
But in his eyes so bright, a song
Does bloom to any man who dares to look.

The song is glad, but full of sorrow,
It's short but long, and owned but borrowed,
It has no meaning and has no end,
An artist with such talent must lend
To maybe a friend?

'Man who dwells to see me,
Man who dwells new light,
Man who seeks dark sorrow,
Make your darkness bright!
But in the centre of your heart,
May there be an endless flight!'

And every man who sees this poem is gone, lost forever . . .

Rosemary Antcliff (11)
Rydes Hill Preparatory School

AUTUMN

A utumn is a time of apples and blackberries
Wrapped up in suet pastry for a pie that is cooking
Gently in the oven for dessert.

U nder your feet are crunching leaves that have fallen quickly
From the bare trees that wave in the wind, howling wildly.

T ouching the conkers on the prickly, sharp, ferocious spikes
                                         on the skin.
I get ready to open them up to see what's inside, when I get home.

U nder the trees are leaves, brown, yellow, orange and red,
Russet, green and crimson, these are the colours of autumn.

M igrating geese, honking on their way to go south for winter,
Going up in the sky past the blazing red sun.

N ow I will smell the smell of chestnuts roasting in the streets.
I buy a few and taste the crunching in my mouth.

Amy Bibbs (10)
Rydes Hill Preparatory School

THE TRAVELLER

The traveller fell and stumbled,
Through the forest, slipping like a drunken man
The yelps of dogs suddenly fell as silent as a grave,
The traveller stopped.
An owl hooted overhead, the sound rippled through the trees,
Gently, like a spirit.
The traveller's face was gaunt,
His eyes were grey and expressionless
Where they had been blue and sparkling like crackers.
He started at the sound of his own footsteps
And he walked like the living dead
He felt the presence behind him and he spun round;
The man grabbed his hands and twisted them behind his back,
He saw the bloated, ugly, sinister face grin,
Seconds before an agonising pain ripped through him.
Like a snake,
Weaving a path of suffering through his veins.

Melissa Benson (11)
Rydes Hill Preparatory School

TO GET A DRINK

I walk and walk
Just walk for hours
The well is still invisible to my weary eyes
I wonder if I have strayed from the path, beaten by tired feet.
My feet bare, burning, bleeding
Ahead, a glimpse of hope glitters through the pain I feel
I begin to run to grab it before it disappears
But it does not
The clay pot plunges into the dark crystal waters
If it does not return, my family will surely die
Splosh! The pot emerges from the silky darkness
Brimming with the lifesaving potion, water
What I wouldn't give to be able to flick a switch
And be fountained with nature's finest wine
Now to commence the endless trek back home
Hours more, now that my pot is full
The speck on the horizon grows
A grape, an apple, a grapefruit, a watermelon
All the while my arms hang against my sides like limp weights
Burdened with my treasure
My hands are blistering
I finally reach home
And I drink deeply.

Isabel Milford (11)
Rydes Hill Preparatory School

AUTUMN

A   Amber leaves layer the ground like a golden carpet,
     Rustling, crunching, crackling as we walk on them.

U   Under the golden leaves animals lie asleep in the warm
     Waiting, waiting for the spring to come.

T   The rain, pattering down on the trees,
     Causing the last of the leaves to fall
     Floating gently towards the ground.

U   Under the dripping trees, people gather chestnuts
     To take home and roast on their cosy fires
     While out here in the cold, squirrels fight to find the last of them.

M   Mornings, the cold, misty, dewy mornings
     Bring a crisp, sharp coldness that is only found in autumn.

N   Now the birds and geese are migrating,
     Honking, cawing, the soft swish of the wings
     As they gently soar through the air.

Iris Brember (11)
Rydes Hill Preparatory School

THE MATCH

A sparkling flame jumps up,
Dazzling, fizzing, wearing a white robe
It frolics about, jumping and gesticulating.
An abundance of beautiful colours burning brightly.

A fiery finger of flame licks about
Glowing ember dances, prancing
Fiercely hot.
A black robe then draws over.

A charred dead body of the match lies still
In darkness, perished, withered and extinct
A chain of darkness lurks.
It is as dead as a doornail
Cowering, it sleeps forever.

Helena Thompson (10)
Rydes Hill Preparatory School

AUTUMN

A Amber, crimson, golden and red
The trees, full of colour, gaily fluttering in the wind
Like a parading pageant.

U Under the golden carpet lie animals huddled up,
Warmed by the bright pattern, floating down from above.

T The wives are making glorious apple and blackberry pies
Made specially for the farmers who live tough and hardy lives.

U Under the misty skies chestnuts roast merrily
As bonfires blaze alight.
For now is the season of Guy Fawkes where fireworks are set alight.

M Migrating graceful geese are flying,
Flying gently over a changing land,
For winter soon is coming to rule a frozen land.

N Now the golden sheaves have been gathered and stored snugly
For the coming winter now on its way.

Rosalind Stonham (11)
Rydes Hill Preparatory School

WATER ON OUR PLANET

H_2O is running out
Some people have to carry six litres a day!
We have to get rid of typhoid, dysentery and cholera - Now!
We need to stop the heartbreak of carrying water every day!
We need to stop acid rain killing our trees!
We have to save our planet - not kill it.
We cannot waste most of our food we should start sharing it evenly.
Start recycling more things.
Say *no* to incinerators which pollute the Earth's atmosphere.
If we can't stop this mayhem, I will have to try and save it - Myself!

Katherine Thomson (12)
Rydes Hill Preparatory School

THE MATCH

The match was struck as a white robe engulfed it.
Slowly creeping down the innocent stick of wood,
As it dances along sparkling and sizzling,
A hot furnace of glowing embers is the fierce flame.

A black, crippled, withering stick, charred and extinguished.
The poor black smoky child scrambles along the path
Of the dead graveyard, lost in the wilderness of darkness.
The match is dead!

Katherine Elsom (11)
Rydes Hill Preparatory School

AUTUMN TERM

The colours of autumn once again.
Brown, gold, crimson, orange, yellow and blue.
The sound of all the noisy geese honking.
The air is so damp and moist.

Roasting hot chestnuts on big crackling bonfires.
Suet pastries and fat, juicy blackberries.
Autumn leaves beneath your warm, cosy feet.
Crunching, crackling and rustling.

Glistening water in the river.
Trickling over so slow.
The slight frost blocks a path.
The water . . . over you go.

The hues in the leaves.
The thick mist on the hillside.
The leaves dance and flutter.
On the misty hillside.

The wind howling and whistling.
Lifting the leaves from the ground.
At the end of the day the sky turns orange, red.
And turns into a sunset!

Emma-Lisa Stephen (11)
Rydes Hill Preparatory School

THE LONE TRAVELLER

Softly, silently striding through the
Lone dark woods,
Trying to escape from danger.
No sound is made from the frightened traveller.

He keeps on moving, and on,
Never stopping to see the world pass by.
Like a bolt of flashing lightning.
He goes as quickly and as quietly as a cheetah.

Like a candle flame flickering
Here and there between the trees,
Never dying out.

Suddenly he disappears into the dark night
And is never seen again.

Kelly Giblin (11)
Rydes Hill Preparatory School

AUTUMN

Autumn is yellow
Autumn is brown
Autumn is rustling leaves that lie on the ground.
Crackling, crunching,
Munching, munching,
Juicy blackberries from the fields.
Autumn smells damp and musty
Like old metals so rusty
Burning bonfires smell the burning acorns.

Sophie Eyles (11)
Rydes Hill Preparatory School

THE FLAME

The glowing ember of the light,
As it flickers and dances,
Pirouetting and prancing,
Red as blood,
Jumping and gesticulating like a girl on a trampoline.

Then suddenly *dead!*

As the extinct match sits solemnly on the window sill.
It now sleeps forever,
With a black as night head
It falls into *Hell!*

Olivia Wallers (10)
Rydes Hill Preparatory School

AUTUMN

A   is for autumn, cold and wet
      also known for its dampness in the air

U   is for under, under your feet,
      the sound of the crimson crackling leaves.

T   is for taste, the red apples and purple juicy blackberries
      cooking in the oven.

U   is for undercover, in your house,
      while the rain outside is tipping down.

M   is for mist in the morning
      while in the air, moist, musty and grey
      you can smell the rotting leaves.

N   is for the noise of the howling which is fierce
      and whistling of the wind which makes you shiver with fear.

Michaela Silvester (11)
Rydes Hill Preparatory School

LIGHT TO DARKNESS

A dazzling flame as red as blood
Prances in front of me,
Showing off an abundance of colours,
Giving off a smell of sulphur
Like a devil it is wicked
Bright orange, yellow and red
Glowing ember, it jumps and gesticulates
And two moments later it is dead.
Extinct. Departed. Gone. Passed away.
I only see a lonely match cowering in the darkness.
Its character inanimate. Its personality cold,
Dead, finished.

Jessica Gardetto (10)
Rydes Hill Preparatory School

THE SPARK'S STORY

In a fire cradle I took my first glimpse,
On the 22nd of September 1666
When soon I cried out loud 'I want to be free!'
My brothers and sisters shouted, 'Stay with me.'

I jumped out of the furnace,
As my little brother Ernest,
Wanted to agree
To jump about with me.

I was meant to bake the bread,
But instead I spread and spread!
In a haystack in Pudding Lane
I could see I was causing pain.

Soon I was a raging fire
Growing, growing, high and higher.
And all the people were running madly,
I was hurting them very badly.

Buckets and buckets and buckets more
Were chasing me across the scarred black floor,
Bit by bit I disappeared,
Till this day I am hiding here
To tell this story of that fire-damaged year.

Jenny Appleby & Hannah Gribble (9)
Rydes Hill Preparatory School

THE SPANISH ARMADA

In the year of 1588,
    The Spanish fleet set out in hate.

The Protestant country of which they were sick,
    Wanted to turn it to Catholic.

The leader - King Philip II of Spain,
    Wanted to conquer Queen Elizabeth's reign.

He gathered many men who would have to fight,
    Who had lots of courage and bagfuls of might.

Through shouting voices 'Man the deck!'
    While other boats sank, burn and wrecked.

Fire ships were sent to kill and burn,
    Firing cannons - they took it in turn.

Many men's lives were lost that day,
    As in the fight the boats did sway.

The rains, hail and wind's great force
    Then drove the Spanish fleet off their course.

The storms made them travel through the cold North Sea,
    They were not very pleased - they were not happy.

Only sixty ships returned to their port,
    And all the ships that had been bought,
        Were ruined in that
            Spanish Armada!

Madeline Benson (9) & Florence Clarke (10)
Rydes Hill Preparatory School

GIRL'S DIARY

In a room, scarce food
All enemy, no friend
Night and day
Just live and pray.
We know from one girl's diary.

Looking down across the street
Cold room, money short.
Diary with a lock and key
Holds the answers of history.
Jews will thank her now.

German soldiers rushing around
Whole family make no sound
One special girl with a story to tell
But no dream that she would be heard
Many years from now.

Her friend, the diary, in her lap
Anne Frank just sat and sat.
Her country suffered, her family hid
Write in that diary is all she did
Until they took her away.

Olivia Johnson (9)
Rydes Hill Preparatory School

EYAM THE FAMOUS PLAGUE VILLAGE

There once lived a tailor in Eyam
Who became very sick with the plague.
He had been very busy with his cloth
Some red, some blue, some beige.

He sent for more from London
To be sent to him at Eyam.
Little did the tailor know
The cloth would very soon kill him.

He touched this cloth, then cuddled his wife
Who gave it to the babes in the pram.
Very soon after that, I'm sad to say
It infected the whole of Eyam.

Soon the plague began to be passed around
So a priest held a meeting and said
'Now my friends you have got this terrible plague
We really must not let it spread.'

So the villagers all stayed where they were,
They didn't decide to leave.
The disease didn't spread, it was kept in check
Just as the priest had said.

Lucinda Wyn-Griffiths (10)
Rydes Hill Preparatory School

THE FIRST CHRISTMAS

A baby in a manger,
In Bethlehem one night,
And shepherds all around him,
And a star shining bright.

A baby in a manger,
And Prince of Heaven and Earth,
A baby in a manger,
This was a miracle birth.

A baby in a manger,
Escapes from Herod the King,
His mother Mary watches,
And a choir of angels sing.

A baby in a manger,
Kings come from lands afar,
A baby in a manger,
They followed the Christmas star.

Louise Fuller (10)
Rydes Hill Preparatory School

THE GARDEN OF EDEN

They who lay in the garden of ease,
They are named Adam and Eve.
They who lay there bare,
With no food or care.
They who God told to beware,
But they turned away,
And went astray.

A mean serpent found Eve in this garden so sweet,
He found a deadly apple and made her eat.
God had said not to eat the fruit of that tree,
So Eve was worried and said
'Good gracious me!'

Adam thought about the fruit and he was curious,
While up above God was furious.
They weren't allowed in the garden again,
Oh the pleasure! Oh the pain!

Hannah Lipinski (10)
Rydes Hill Preparatory School

ANTARCTICA

In the winter there lies below,
A group of penguins huddled so low,
In whirling winds and icy snow.
The seals all dance in the sea below.

In the summer the penguins squawk,
And waddle around in penguin walk,
The blue whales sing in blue whale talk,
They dance about like the ork.

Elizabeth Elsom (9)
Rydes Hill Preparatory School

ANTARCTICA

Cold and dark as lead
Winter!
Snow softly but quickly falls
Seas emerald green and awfully deep
Great gales lie ahead of those who live there
'But where?' they call
In Antarctica, Antarctica
Where animals live and feed
Penguins and birds you see
In Antarctica, Antarctica
Where fog comes pouring in
Rays of sun glittering on the snow
Summer!
Where penguins dance all night and day
And where whales dive and sing their lonely song
In Antarctica, Antarctica.

Alice Antcliff (8)
Rydes Hill Preparatory School

ANTARCTICA

In the lonely lands of Antarctica,
Icicles hang high and low and
Icebergs drift.
Antarctica's snowy lands,
Glow in the midnight sun with the flickering lights.
A group of penguins silhouetted on the horizon,
The icy waters of the ocean lie calm,
A calling of penguins breaks the silence,
They are looking for their young,
A seal dances through deep shadows of the ocean.

Helen Pearson (8)
Rydes Hill Preparatory School

ANTARCTICA

Antarctica is a lovely place
The seabirds gliding full of grace
The weather is cold and blustery too
It feels lonely with nobody with you
It is too cold to live there
But animals live there somewhere
The cracking ice and windy sea
I wish you were here to be with me

The icebergs are a danger to ships,
But the big blue whale does his beautiful flips
The ice floats on the sea so grand
As the penguins call to their children on land
The snow sparkles like glitter on your face
In the magical world of Antarctica.

Hannah Reid (9)
Rydes Hill Preparatory School

ANTARCTICA

The sparkling landscape all covered in snow,
The freezing sunshine dazzling and clear,
Still, stark, bright blue sky,
The twilight and the midnight sun.

The starless sky,
The freezing ice,
The song of the whales
The seals dance in a watery paradise.

Isabelle Edmondson (8)
Rydes Hill Preparatory School

ANTARCTICA

The frostiness of the ice,
The hardness of the sleet.
The howling wind,
The blistering cold.
The storms that will break you to bits,
The fogginess that will make you feel blind.
The violent wind,
The friendless birds on the icy sea.
That's what Antarctica is like!

Hope Allen (8)
Rydes Hill Preparatory School

ANTARCTICA

Antarctica is freezing,
It's cold and you feel the howling wind
The seals are doing ballet,
The penguins snapping to find food,
Antarctica is covered in white snow,
Seas bang against the rocks.

Lauren Silvester (8)
Rydes Hill Preparatory School

ANTARCTIC POEM

In the winter the blizzards howl,
It is snowy, stormy and violent,
The loneliness is horrid,
But it is dull and alone.
The winters are long and lonely.

The summers are short and bright.
The azure skies,
The dazzling, dreamy and beautiful snow,
But the sun never sets,
In this land of the midnight sun.

In the Antarctic the animals lie,
Untamed, wild and free,
But very few types of animals,
Live there.

Lucy Porter (9)
Rydes Hill Preparatory School

ANTARCTIC

In winter it is terribly cold,
When you step right out of your door
You'll get a whip right on your cheek
The wind, the hail and all the storms
It pulls you back alone,
The animals are cold in the freezing snow,
The animals catching their prey,
They're covered in lovely white snow,
The penguins feed from their mothers
Then go away
The humpbacks turn in the dark blue ocean
Catching their prey as they go.

It's summer, it's still cold weather
There's a rainbow in the cold blue sky,
The nature and the sunshine,
And every animal is very pleased,
The starlight express in the dark blue sky
At night-time every night.

Philippa Robinson (9)
Rydes Hill Preparatory School

ANTARCTICA

Through the misty whirlwind.
Lies Antarctica.
It's neglected and friendless.
For no one lives there.

Down under the deep, mysterious sea.
Live whales and seals.
And sometimes even squabbling penguins.
That's what lives under the sea.

Harriet Carne (9)
Rydes Hill Preparatory School

ANTARCTICA

Whipped winds blow from the icy sea,
Mist and fog block the view,
Drizzly snow falls from above,
While down below a draught will blow,
Storms that come are violent,
Sweeping the snow to a different place,
Cracking the ice to a jigsaw puzzle,
Blowing the sea to a boisterous rage.

Standing solitary, penguins huddle,
Diving into the stormy water,
Grabbing krill for the fluffy young,
Finally stopping for the show,
Seals dance twisting and twirling,
Deep in the dark lagoon,
Huge Humpback whales join the party,
Flipping their tails to applaud.

Katharine Jarrold (9)
Rydes Hill Preparatory School

BLUE

Blue is the sky above my head,
Blue is the sea as calm as my bed.
Upon my head I wear a blue hat,
By the back door is a blue mat.
Bluebells ringing at the strike of moonlight.
Sapphire ring shining in the starlight.
Fireworks shooting to the moon!
And coming down all too soon.
Colours of crayons and my hairband,
I painted a blue hand.

Rebecca Beasley (7)
Rydes Hill Preparatory School

GREEN

Green is a peppermint in a bag,
Green are the stripes on a flag.
Lettuce is a vegetable that I eat,
And grapes are a fruit that are sweet.
Green is ivy crawling up the trees,
Green are the leaves trembling in the breeze.
Green is a flutter that comes in spring,
And green is a parrot with two wings.
Green is a grasshopper jumping around,
And green is a dress pretty and round.

Charlotte Graham-Moss (8)
Rydes Hill Preparatory School

ORANGE

Orange is a ginger cat,
Or a feather on a hat.
Orange is a juicy mango,
Also the colour of the tango.
Orange is the sunset sky,
For bright flowers when people die.
Orange is marmalade and jam,
And for volcano when it goes bang.
Orange is a fire at night,
A pumpkin at Hallowe'en - What a fright!

Cerys A Jenkins (8)
Rydes Hill Preparatory School

BLUE POEM

Blue is the colour of the lake
Blue is the colour of the drakes
Blue is the colour of the high sky
Blue is the colour of a fly
Blue is the colour of spooky houses
Blue is the colour of blue trousers
Blue is the colour of blue balloons
Blue is the colour of blue pantaloons
Blue is for bluebirds
Blue is for blue words.

Susanna Salmon (7)
Rydes Hill Preparatory School

BLACK

Black is for sky in the night,
Black is for cat sneaking out of sight.
Black is for boot kicking away,
Black is for clothes that you wear in the day.
Black is for the ink in your pen,
Black is for bowler hat on the head of men.
Black is for bag that you hold in your hand,
Black is for hair that you can tie in a band.
Black is for clouds in a thunderstorm,
Black is for car blowing a horn.

Sophie Reid (8)
Rydes Hill Preparatory School

ORANGE

Orange is for fireworks spinning high,
Orange is for fire dancing in the sky.
Orange is for carrots popping out of the ground,
Orange is for pumpkins at Hallowe'en when the witches come round.
Orange is for oranges sitting there all sad,
Orange is for tigers growling like mad.
Orange is for paint when people paint on the wall,
Orange is for dress hanging on a stall.
Orange is for chalk when we write on the board,
Orange is for flower beautiful but ignored.

Helen Childs (7)
Rydes Hill Preparatory School

TELEVISION

Television is the best thing
Record breaking girl thing
Disney is my favourite channel
Me, Zoe and Dad are the best TV panel
Excellent funny shows it really goes
Good fun to watch but at bedtime
It has to stop.

Kim Nicholls (7)
St Bartholomew's CE Primary School, Haslemere

MY CAT

My cat goes on my bed
He follows me in the shed
He's down the stairs
And he always glares.

My cat likes to play
He runs up the stairs all the way,
He likes to drink milk
He likes sleeping on silk.

Edward Rofe (9)
St Bartholomew's CE Primary School, Haslemere

SKATEBOARDING

This is an easy thing to learn
You need a board to ride
It's a sporty thing to do
I have a board to ride.

I can ride down a ramp and do tricks
And I can ride home every day
I can do kick flip
And I practice every day.

Christopher Barnes (8)
St Bartholomew's CE Primary School, Haslemere

THE COW

The friendly cow all red and white,
I love her with all my heart.
She gives me cream with all her might,
To eat an apple tart.

As the night falls the wind goes by,
She walks along the pigsty.
And says goodnight for today,
And goes to lie down on the hay.

As the night turns to day,
The friendly cow gets off the hay.
And down come the showers,
She walks along the meadow grass
And eats the meadow flowers.

Laura Cavannagh (7)
St Bartholomew's CE Primary School, Haslemere

SEALIFE

I like sealife
Because I like seeing the fish
In a school swimming together.

I watch big groups of fish together
And their different colours stand out through the moving sea.

The dolphins popping up,
Through the waves give you a shock
But it is a lovely sight.

Kate Short (7)
St Bartholomew's CE Primary School, Haslemere

DOWN IN THE SEA

Sometimes the sun glitters on the sea,
I wish a dolphin went swimming with me.
Lots of dolphins splashing near the shore,
Tons of people clapping for more.
Squelchy seaweed on the ground,
Lots of dogfish in the pound.

Hannah Rose (8)
St Bartholomew's CE Primary School, Haslemere

THE MEAT EATER

It's hiding in the grass
Its gleaming claws are waiting for a kill,
It's started running
The legs are fast.
And its gleaming eye
Has spotted the kill.
It has the bite it has waited for,
The bite that saved its life.

Clive Hogan (8)
St Bartholomew's CE Primary School, Haslemere

THE SEASIDE

I watched waves splashing over the sparkling sand,
Crabs crawling out of band.
I saw jellyfish stinging toes
And a baby wearing no clothes.
Children were playing with a rubber ring
And I sat down and listened to the skylarks sing.

Flora Day
St Bartholomew's CE Primary School, Haslemere

ELECTRICITY

Electricity, electricity,
What is electricity useful for?
Electricity is useful for nearly everything.
Electricity, electricity,
Is electricity dangerous?
Electricity is dangerous to touch
Because you might get a shock.
Electricity, electricity,
I think I like electricity but sometimes
I forget that electricity is hot.

Beth Crudgington (9)
St Bartholomew's CE Primary School, Haslemere

ALIEN

There's an alien in my garden,
It lives in a shed,
It came from Mars.
It likes bread,
It lives on chocolate bars!

Thomas Moore (8)
St Bartholomew's CE Primary School, Haslemere

HORSES

Horses, horses galloping through the moss,
Wading through the river
The stepping stones they don't need to cross.
Nibbling at the flowers, jumping the fences,
People who have glasses can't believe they're there
And polish their lenses.
Rearing, bucking, biting, kicking, fighting
All wild ponies do those things
Most people think they're horrible
But I love ponies.

Nathalie Badger (8)
St Bartholomew's CE Primary School, Haslemere

MY CAT

My cat always glares
Going down the stairs.
My cat is very furry
And he's even very hairy.
My cat always purrs
And his eyes look blurry.

Andrew Scattergood (9)
St Bartholomew's CE Primary School, Haslemere

ARACHNOPHOBIA

I heard some shrieking down the hall,
A swarm of spiders on the wall,
I got a glass, I got a hammer,
I got some nails and a spanner,
I ran downstairs and told my dad,
'A horrible dream,' he said I'd had.

Up to the room, with all my tools,
My dad and mum told me the rules,
I opened the door but spiders came at me,
I locked the door and took the key
Then a little spider, small and thin
Came crawling through the door within.

I screamed, I ran as more came through
My mum shouted out 'What's wrong with you?'
I muttered, 'Spiders,' and ran upstairs,
Mouldy skin beneath the hairs,
I tried to keep my teeth from chattering,
I looked through the window and heard some
Clattering . . . !

Polly Lomas (8)
St Bartholomew's CE Primary School, Haslemere

A CAT

A cat is furry,
A cat walks on air.
A cat is lazy,
A cat sleeps on a chair.
A cat climbs the fence,
A cat does a dance.

Daniel Dillon-Thiselton (8)
St Bartholomew's CE Primary School, Haslemere

THE KEY TO THE CASTLE

In the cellar cold and bare,
Dark as a grave with nobody there,
Sat a spider huge and fat,
Who wove her web and sat and sat,
On top of the box,
With the rusty locks,
That holds the key to the castle.

Down the stairs that rumble and creak,
Where every small step moans and squeaks,
Down to the cellar cold and bare,
Dark as a grave with nobody there,
Sat a spider huge and fat,
Who wove her web and sat and sat,
On top of the box,
With the rusty locks,
That holds the key to the castle.

Past the rat with the yellow teeth,
Sharp as sorrow and long as grief,
Who ran up the creaking, crumbling stair,
Up from the cellar cold and bare,
Dark as a grave with nobody there,
Except the spider huge and fat,
Who wove her web and sat and sat,
On top of the box,
With the rusty locks,
That holds the key to the castle.

Jessica Akers (8)
St Bartholomew's CE Primary School, Haslemere

FEAR

A dread dangles above our heads,
 I barely gamble to think,
Of the awful gate that each one dreads,
 From which the bravest shrink.
It's not the destroying shrapnel shell,
 It's not the sniper's plot.
It's not machine-gun's burst of Hell,
 It's not these that matter a jot.
It's a far worse thing than that, my mate,
 With which we have to grapple,
It is we see our own worst fate,
 Ration tins of plum and apple.

Allen Tillyard (9)
St Bartholomew's CE Primary School, Haslemere

THE DRAGON

The dragon can breathe out fire
Red-hot burning fire,
Burning away at anything.

The dragon can lash with its tail
A very long, thick, chunky tail,
Smashing and crashing away.

The dragon has a bad temper,
A temper that's very explosive
That could go off at any time.

The dragon has big wings
Scaly wings to carry,
Him about the sky.

The dragon has funny arms
That can be clumsy,
Especially at meals.

The dragon is no more
No more! No more! No more!
Good heavens there's one right behind you!

William Halfhide (10)
St Bartholomew's CE Primary School, Haslemere

MONSTER!

Here is a monster,
He's seven feet tall.
His head made of iron.
And face made from wood.

His feet look like fire,
His legs look like snakes.
His chest made from armour,
That's all it takes.

His eyes look like rabbits,
His nose smells of eggs.
His mouth is so long,
And ears are big pegs.

Alex Ford (10)
St Bartholomew's CE Primary School, Haslemere

MY HOLIDAY

I'm going on my holiday,
I see the dolphins swimming by.
I'm going on my holiday,
The boat is gently swaying.
I'm going on my holiday,
The waves are getting bigger!
I'm going on my holiday,
I'm having second thoughts!
I'm going on my holiday,
Waves come crashing against the boat!
I'm going on my holiday,
Everybody is feeling sick.
I'm going on my holiday,
Suddenly the boat rolls over!
I'm going on my holiday,
I must get out of the boat.
I'm going on my holiday,
I do get out of the boat.
I'm going on my holiday,
I reach dry land at last.
I'm already on my holiday,
My family, not here.
This is not a very nice holiday,
As I fall back into the water.
It was my very last holiday,
The world is over for me.

Jessica Simpson (10)
St Bartholomew's CE Primary School, Haslemere

THE LION HUNT

It's only a penguin,
Splashing about
It's only a tiger,
Waiting for food
It's only a camel,
With three humps
But wait
It's
A
Lion
That was the end of the
Lion hunt.

Ella-Louise Mumford (10)
St Bartholomew's CE Primary School, Haslemere

ELEPHANT SWAYS

There is a big elephant in India,
He sways his long, thick trunk,
Big feet stomping in the long grass,
Out approached a tiger and gave a
Great big roar.

The frightened elephant feels scared,
Then they both walk away from each other,
Elephant sways his trunk,
He stomps to a water fountain
And gulps down a lot of water.

He walks over to a long, thick tree,
Now it's time for a rest,
Back comes the tiger,
And do you know what?
He went to lie down next to the elephant.

Hollie Judic (9)
St Bartholomew's CE Primary School, Haslemere

ALIENS

Look! A signal coming
Right this way
Look! It's still coming
From a million miles away

The people are all running all around the globe
Crying out in hope that
We can launch a probe
All of a sudden they all drop
As the spaceship descends hisses and plop
Aliens.

George Hogan (9)
St Bartholomew's CE Primary School, Haslemere

METAL MONSTER

A metal munching monster, feasting on cogs and bogs,
Munching, crunching, smashing old cars,
Beating, deseating, poor biker-riders,
Crashing, bashing, destroying the junkyard.
Streaking, reeking of bits of old rust,
Dazing, hair-raising, zooming around the place,
Mashing, lashing any kitchen equipment
Thinking of drinking gallons of oil.

William Maisey (9)
St Bartholomew's CE Primary School, Haslemere

THE STRANGER

There was a stranger in the wood,
    About five feet tall and there he stood,
With bright green hair and purple eyes,
    He was the stranger, oh yes he was.

With hands the size of dustbin lids,
    And feet the size of little kids,
You couldn't see his facial features
    Covered with a fluffy beard.

The stranger on that sunny day,
    Packed his bags and went away,
I think I'm going to miss that stranger,
    I hope he comes back in the future.

Hannah Collins (10)
St Bartholomew's CE Primary School, Haslemere

ALTHOUGH I WAS

Although I was one, I learnt to say mama.
Although I was two, I learnt to walk.
Although I was three, I went to somebody's first birthday party.
Although I was four, I learnt to use the toilet.
Although I was five, I got my first bike.
Although I was six, I had my first hair cut.
Although I was seven, I went to Thorpe Park.
Although I was eight, I went to Wacky Warehouse.
Now I am nine, I had a great birthday.

Carrey Renmant (9)
St Bartholomew's CE Primary School, Haslemere

THE FUTURE

The future, it's hard to explain what I think.
Spacecraft, floating houses that fly,
We might even live on a different planet,
We might not even have to blink,
The sea might turn red, the land might turn blue!
But I'm not sure, in fact I haven't really got a clue,

What will we drive in?
How will we eat?
What will our houses look like?
How will we compete?

Well, this is my imagination,
It's what I believe,
So next time you have a chance,
Open up your imagination
And see what you conceive.

Roman Flourendzou (10}
St Bartholomew's CE Primary School, Haslemere

WHAT IT'S LIKE IN THE DARK

The sun went down
The moon came up
The stars sparkled like jewels
The lakes were still as ice
That glistened in the dark
The trees blew in the strong wind
And the dustbin lids rattle
People meander home after work
Some curtains shut really tight
People put lots of logs on the fire.
I snuggle down in my cosy bed
And wrap my duvet around my neck
The last of the embers of the fire are gone
I shut my eyes and wait for dawn.

Eleanor MacDonald (9)
St Bartholomew's CE Primary School, Haslemere

THE OCEAN

Thick misty blue ocean moving swiftly.
Free to be its own master.
It's as warm as fire or as cold as ice!
It swerves and sways all around the earth,
Turning into thick ice and melting once more.
The ocean is full of life forms
That have never been discovered before.
The ocean is a puzzle of water and life.

Matthew Varney (10)
St Bartholomew's CE Primary School, Haslemere

ADVENTURES IN MY LIFE

At one, I swallowed a plum,
When two, my face turned blue,
Then three, I went on a ride, wee!
And four, I opened a door,
At five, I thought I'd survive,
When six, my teacher gave me ticks,
Then seven, I believed in Heaven,
At eight, I could stay up late,
But when nine, my nan went blind!
And now ten, I can see Big Ben.

Matthew Nash (10)
St Bartholomew's CE Primary School, Haslemere

PEOPLE

People come in different
Sizes and shapes,
People are tall
And some are small,
People are fat
People are thin,
People walk and talk,
People are old
People are young,
People have cars
And some fly to Mars,
People are strong,
People are weak,
People are good,
People are bad
And some get very mad,
People like to
Read Harry Potter books,
And girls are good looks.

Richard Barnes (10)
St Bartholomew's CE Primary School, Haslemere

MY CAT BLOSSOM

I got her for my sixth birthday
She was really cute and fluffy
Mostly grey with a white and ginger tummy
And white tip on her tail.

    Her pink nose reminded me of a blossom bud
    So, I called her Blossom.
    Blossom had a loud purr and if I couldn't find her
    I just had to listen for her purring.

One day when I came home from school
Blossom had had five kittens.
There were three grey ones,
A marmalade colour and a black one.

    We had to give away all her kittens
    Because we already had two cats.
    This made me very sad and Blossom too.

When we go back home
I would really like another cat for my own.
I really loved my cat Blossom.

Victoria Shier (10)
St Bartholomew's CE Primary School, Haslemere

GARGOYLES

Dangling from buildings
With their evil eyes and
Spouts pouring water,
Death in the air.
Thick black smoke and
Making howling sounds
But silent,
Careless of the world below.
Ugly creatures,
Lurking in the distance,
Waiting for the kill.
As they wait
Gloom mists swirl around.
Then morning rises.
Now all is well . . .

Natalie Hill (8)
St Bartholomew's CE Primary School, Haslemere

MYSTICAL, MAGICAL GARGOYLES

Mystical gargoyles, peering from behind the wall.
You have not seen them, they hide.
Such is their habit, not to be seen,
Terribly ugly, face all twisted.
In the moonlight the face changes
Catching the light on his mouth.
A magical gargoyle he is,
Lovely, mystical and magical.

Magically moving, slow and silently
As the moon goes by. Some
Gargoyles are sleeping.
It is dawn
Creeping round the chimneys.
Around the buildings.
Laughing, sit the gargoyles:

Mystical, magical gargoyles . . .

Zoe Julie Nicholls (8)
St Bartholomew's CE Primary School, Haslemere

GARGOYLES

Scary, secret gargoyles
Scare off evil spirits

Gruesome, grisly gargoyles
Frightening in the gloom

Mysterious, mask-like
Gargoyles
Are wicked water spouts

Ugly, unnatural gargoyles
An unforgettable sight.

Matthew Putnam (8)
St Bartholomew's CE Primary School, Haslemere

GARGOYLES

Gargoyles are ugly, old and fat
Arrogant and selfish
Ruder than a rat
Greedy and mean
Often looks down
Yawning broad and wide,
Laughing loud and clear.
Everybody hates them . . .
Sun comes up as dawn awakes and gargoyles are
Sleeping sleeping . . .

Elspeth May Alexander (8)
St Bartholomew's CE Primary School, Haslemere

THE FIRST SAMURAI

In the land of old Japan
Lived a boy called Ghun Hoy
He loved to eat papaya in a can
With a bowl of shan poy
The papaya was really very sweet
And he ate it out of bamboo
He only got it as a treat
And he got enough for two.
After a year he decided to join the army
So he had to buy a sword
He bought the pan yamy
It looked better than an award

Then he got bamboo
And cut it all in half
Then he made some armour (starting with the shoe)
But he slipped and cut his calf
He finished his armour 100% complete
He put on his father's helmet
It really was quite neat
He decided to eat some ken yet
For energy as the first Samurai.

Kyle Kapur (11)
St Bartholomew's CE Primary School, Haslemere

THE MONSTER

He lived at the top of a rocky, old cliff,
His face was so gruesome,
His skin was so stiff,
His feet were all rotten,
His nails overgrown,
To the people of this world,
He was never shown,
They say his heart was so cold,
So cold his touch would give you frostbite,
He was so ghastly and gruesome,
Such a terrible, frightening sight.

Katherine Jones (10)
St Bartholomew's CE Primary School, Haslemere

THERE WAS AN OLD MAN FROM BEL AIR

There was an old man from Bel Air,
Who was chased by a rampaging bear,
He ran up a tree,
Said, '1, 2, 3,
Clear off or I'll shoot my gun,'
So the bear started to run.

Later that night,
When there was no light,
The man was still in the tree.
The bear had come back,
And was ready to attack.
But the man wanted to plea,
And bowed his head to one knee.

'Oh why, oh why you silly bear,
Are you standing right down there.'
Answered the bear, 'I want to eat you,
Even though you're covered in tree glue.'
So said the man, 'Yes, oh yes you cannot get me,
Up in this old sticky Tibet tree.'

It was the middle of the day,
And the man was nearly away.
He slid down the bark,
'Down there looks quite dark.'
And went right into the tummy of the bear,
That dead old man from Bel Air.

Frederick Lomas (11)
St Bartholomew's CE Primary School, Haslemere

SCHOOL IS GREAT

Assemblies I could do without,
The best bit is giving hymn books out.

Playing football gives me a stitch,
But I'd miss my lessons marking the pitch.

Art, you draw sculptures,
Such as wicked witches
And flying vultures.

PE is so boring you jump over benches and that,
You jump over horses and gravity as forces
And land on a baby-blue mat.

Story time about a sandy beach bay,
Though I'd rather be putting the rubbish away.

School is really great - but
I'll tell you what,
Going home beats the lot!

Emma Webb (11)
St Bartholomew's CE Primary School, Haslemere

SPACE

I'd like to go into outer space,
And wander round in total grace,
I'd flap my wings and pass the moon
Or tootle round in a gold balloon.
I'd swim through nothing to the sun -
That's where I'd have all the fun.
I'd take a photo of a planet
(A new one made of shiny granite)
Meet an alien called Felaxy
While hanging about in a tourist galaxy.
Then I'd watch a headless troll,
Jump into an endless black-hole.
Then go back to my place of birth,
What's that planet? Oh yeah, Earth.
When I'm there see a star,
And say to myself, 'I've been that far.'
Just before that visit a Milky Way,
But I think I'll just stay here today!

Becca Bromley (10)
St Bartholomew's CE Primary School, Haslemere

WHAT WILL I BE

Every time I watch TV,
My mum comes in and stares at me,
She looks at me in such a way
That I know what she is thinking.
She's thinking 'What will you be?'
Perhaps I'll be a nurse, a doctor or a vet,
It's very hard to know I haven't
Thought about it yet.
I may be a policewoman at the scene of a crime,
Or even a poet thinking of a rhyme.
But, in reality, nobody knows
What I will be,

Not even
Me!

Scarlett Robertson (10)
St Bartholomew's CE Primary School, Haslemere

MUSIC

Music is such a beautiful thing,
It sometimes makes you dance or sing.

Rocky or jazzy or really calm,
It can sometimes act quite like a balm.

It puts you to sleep and takes you away
And can leave you to dream 'til the end of the day.

I think music is really great,
And if it was a man, he'd be my best mate.

Olivia Cauley (10)
St Bartholomew's CE Primary School, Haslemere

OUR FOUR SEASONS

Spring

Spring is a time for all things new,
The weather is changing, the sky is blue.
The fields are green and lambs can be seen,
This is the way it's always been.

Summer

Though I prefer the summertime,
There's lemon to drink with a slice of lime.
The sun in the sky glowing all day long,
The birds in the tree break into a song.

Autumn

Why was the wind so bad those days?
Rain fell to the ground in all kinds of ways.
Sometimes spitting with a wind so spiteful,
But that's the autumn, not at all delightful.

Winter

Snowdrops falling down to the ground,
Spinning and twirling round and round.
My fingers feel green, my feet feel blue,
My face feels cold and my legs do too.

Kate Jones (10)
St Bartholomew's CE Primary School, Haslemere

THE OLD MAN FROM BILBAO, WHO ATE A COW

There once was a man from Bilbao,
Who once or twice ate a cow,
These one or two,
His friends all knew,
Could cost him his life,
So they told his wife!

His wife understood,
And did all she could,
To tell his old mother,
Then his dear brother,
Soon all people had heard the news,
So farmers began to accuse!

'You fat, ugly hound,
Confusion's all around,
You've stolen my stock,
The best of my flock,
No, a flock's full of sheep,
But cattle's what I keep!'

The old man took it badly,
Stormed out the house madly,
He ran across a desert,
Like a fox chasing a leveret,
Then he stumbled and fell,
On the sand plains he died well!

The family wept,
His body they kept,
And still today,
There's a chance that you may,
Find what he found,
For no less that five pound! *(Beef steak!)*

Matthew Hitchmough (10)
St Bartholomew's CE Primary School, Haslemere

UNDER THE BED

Under the bed lies a gruesome, frightening monster,
    What does it look like I wonder?
His lime green hair and lemon yellow face stands out
Between its frightening fangs,
'Am I being stupid?' Yes, my head says.
Under the covers, listening all the time,
Was that a scratch, or is it just fine.
I peer over the bed, a glistening claw draws out
Is it just my mind, or is the monster about,
Out it suddenly pounces, ready for the kill,
It sprints across the room, leaping for the window sill,
Oh, it's just the cat, everything's fine,
Or is the monster still there waiting for the right time.

Thomas Alvarez (10)
St Bartholomew's CE Primary School, Haslemere

HOLIDAY

The last day of term, the school bell does a single ring,
The shouts of voices as the children sing,
The mums draw up their cars, and the children depart
Not coming to school for many a day,
But for the teachers it's not all fun and play,
Marking books, far away,
Do the children care? No, they're on holiday.

The next day they have a lie-in,
And escape from school's noisy din,
Ask the neighbour where the Smiths are today,
'They've gone to the USA,' they say.
Myself I go out to play,
On a lovely, hot sunny day,
This is because they're on holiday.

It's a sunny day, no cares today,
They're on holiday.

Gregory Kent (10)
St Bartholomew's CE Primary School, Haslemere

THE SEASONS

The spring is a time for new life,
Trees start to grow,
Plants start to sprout,
All waiting to see what spring will bring.

Summer is a time for brightness,
A time for light,
The crops are in full flow,
And the days are so long.

Autumn is when all the trees have lost their leaves,
And migrant birds have flown far away to warmer climes,
With frosty mornings and cold nights.

Winter is when plants wither and die,
With an ever threat of snow,
And long cold nights and short days,
Winter migrants arrive coming from colder climates,

Spring is my favourite season,
What's yours?

Anthony Moodie (10)
St Bartholomew's CE Primary School, Haslemere

THE MADMAN OF BABU

There was once a man from Babu
Who managed to burn up a shoe.
It was considered a sin
By the bloke down the inn.
And the landlord asked what, why and who?

David Short (10)
St Bartholomew's CE Primary School, Haslemere

SEASONS

Spring will soon be here
With all the flowers
Coming through
Crocuses and daffodils to name but a few.
Summer is next with warm sunshine
A visit to the seaside is just fun
Holidays are great with lots of
Fun and plenty to do
Then comes autumn with all
The changing colours
Yellow, reds and oranges too.
Then there's winter
The weather chills us
And Jack Frost goes where
He thinks he will.

Danielle Walters (10)
St Bartholomew's CE Primary School, Haslemere

MY BEST FRIEND

My *best* friend she's so neat
She's a really good singer,
And a really cool swinger.
She's so kind with her brainy mind,
Like a daydream you just want to find.

Claire Andow (11)
St Bartholomew's CE Primary School, Haslemere

BONFIRE NIGHT

Sitting there alone dry twigs and leaves,
Waiting there for the soon to come audience,
In the distance footsteps coming,
Now the fire is lit and the yellow, red, and orange warmth comes out
Of the blaze. After two hours of a fire blazing,
You can see the fire crack as it dies,
The fire falls to ash and the footsteps fade into the darkness.

David Addison (10)
St Bartholomew's CE Primary School, Haslemere

FRIENDS!

This is what a friend should be:
Kind and gentle, as funny as me.
Also they should listen, when things have gone all wrong,
And to cheer you up maybe even sing a little song.
But you see, my friend and me, we had a little tiff.
And me and her, we both began to sniff.
I said to her:
'We're doing this all wrong.
Best friends are supposed to stand big and bold and strong'.

Elli Stracey (10)
St Bartholomew's CE Primary School, Haslemere

FIREWORKS

Boom, sizzle, crackle, bang!
These are the sounds of fireworks,
Boom, sizzle, crackle, bang!
Watch them sizzle and start to fizzle.

Boom, sizzle, crackle, bang!
Watch that one start to explode,
Listen to the piercing screech!
Boom, sizzle, crackle, bang!

Boom, sizzle, crackle, bang!
Who thinks fireworks are fun?

Mark Rofe (11)
St Bartholomew's CE Primary School, Haslemere

THE UNTOUCHED CARPET

The untouched carpet of soft white powder
Lies frozen on the ground
The multicoloured burning sky
Lit up by the dark red sun
It goes melting down like a candle in full flame
With the sweet music of birds singing
In the silence of the bewildering plains

The dissolving light hiding itself away
After the stretching hills that stay,
Beyond the reach of human eye!
The hills that lie lonely and lost
But full of life and never die.

The crunching whiteness scattered on the hills
Have an everlasting glistening touch
The frozen lake, like crystal with such
Beauty and peace and a secret shield
Which seems to hold forever
From all the enemies and unknown strangers
Who come from the towering fields.

Dorothy Klepacka (10)
St Bartholomew's CE Primary School, Haslemere

MY FRIEND

I've got a very best friend,
She's going round the bend.
People think she's weird,
Because she's got a beard.

She's not allowed a dog,
So she brought a little frog.
Her mummy got very mad,
It made her very sad.

She likes to watch the telly,
While stuffing herself with jelly.
Her mother says she'll get square eyes,
If she keeps watching Sky.

That's the end of my little story,
But also the end of my moment of glory.
I've told you my tale,
And I expect by now you're feeling pale.

Kayleigh Barrass (10)
St Bartholomew's CE Primary School, Haslemere

NOAH'S JOURNEY
(The True Version)

The elephants went in two by two,
The skunk, the cat and the kangaroo,
The bee went in and stung the dog,
He tripped in pain and stood on the frog.

The hippos went in four by four,
They were so big they got stuck in the door.
Then they played a game of soccer,
All the animals were off their rocker.
Then Noah came in and he said,
'You behave or you won't be fed.'

Elissa Scott (10)
St Bartholomew's CE Primary School, Haslemere

DOWN I TRAVEL

Down I travel in my car,
Looking out among the stars.
Yet I know it will be a long time,
Till I hear the windmills chime.
So I'll wait in my car
Looking out among the stars.
The air is like a quiet phase;
It's just like a short daze.

Suzanne Gardner (10)
St Bartholomew's CE Primary School, Haslemere

UNDER THE WATER

Under the water swimming along,
Dolphins, sharks and stingrays too,
Travelling along side by side,
On my journey they will come with me.

They will come with me,
They will be by my side, all through the journey.
Until we find a place to hide.

At first they saw me as their lunch,
But now they will come with me,
On my journey under the sea,
They will always be by my side.

Elizabeth Henderson (10)
St Bartholomew's CE Primary School, Haslemere

THE CAPTAIN'S VOYAGE

I sailed across a mighty sea.
It was really strong and blue.

I nearly fell and broke the bell,
Of the mighty captain's crew.

I walked into the cellar,
To see what was down there.

Oh no the captain's gone bare!
He told me what had happened.

I told the rest of the crew,
We sailed across the stormy sea,
Which was getting kind of rough.

We had raced against the pace of the stormy sea.
We got to the land and the crew was happy.

The captain got his clothes back.

That was the end of the captain and his crew!

Sheena Pocock (10)
St Bartholomew's CE Primary School, Haslemere

MY HOMEWORK POEM

Homework, oh homework
I like you so much.
But sometimes it depends
What you are.

Homework, oh homework.
Please be easy for me.
Sometimes writing, sometimes drawing,
Sometimes even reading.

Homework, oh homework.
Of course it is true,
I really do
Like doing you.

Fern Doyle (10)
St Bartholomew's CE Primary School, Haslemere

FITFUL DREAM

I move around, fitfully as I dream.

I scoop up the moon with my chubby hands.

The soldiers on my bed shoot tiny holes in the covers.

I walk around the corner and I freeze.

Was that a witch flying through the trees?

From behind a bush a cat leaps then stares.

What made it jump? What was there?

I woke suddenly, as stiff as a cactus.

I struggled to focus as the sun shone in my half-opened eyes.

I sighed disappointedly,
'It was just a dream!'

James Geer (10)
St Bartholomew's CE Primary School, Haslemere

ON MY OWN

I was on my own, walking down the road.
I thought I was being followed.

The shop was close.
I did not want to go back.

My face was pale.

My hands shook.

My legs like quivering jelly, quivering quickly.

I fell on my knees, as people walked by.

No one helped because they thought I was poor.

Sad people ignoring my journey.

Fiona Culley (10)
St Bartholomew's CE Primary School, Haslemere

TRAVEL THROUGH SPACE

When I travelled through space
I saw a green alien's face.
I landed on Mars.
And saw space cars,
The cars were funny
Shaped as little red bunnies.
Mars was red.
The blue Martians were dead.
Then I went to Saturn,
The aliens were flattened,
And I said to myself,
'They're not in good health.'
I ended my journey, stuck on the moon,
And I have been there ever since June.

Katie Beaven (10)
St Bartholomew's CE Primary School, Haslemere

NIGHT

The night was gloomy as the moon shone
Bright in the darkness of the night.
What could be flying about except for the *big black bat*?
Every night I get the shivers looking out my window.
Suddenly I hear a crash!
What could it be?
What? What?
After a while I fall asleep, dreaming of the *big black bat*!

Lara Martin (10)
St Bartholomew's CE Primary School, Haslemere

JOURNEY OF THOUGHTS

I went on a journey into the woods,
To walk my dog, Ben.
I fed my dog and then we went,
But the dog's lead got a bit bent.
We went
In the shed to find
Some rope just broke.

My voice had a very loud croak,
My dog was scared in sight of a goat,
He ate some thorns and had a sore throat.

My friend called Fred was ill in bed.
So I said, 'I hope you get better soon,'
Ben looked straight into the moon.
It was all dark,
Ben started to bark.

Jade Sheppard (10)
St Bartholomew's CE Primary School, Haslemere

SPACE MISSION '3.14'

The world's going to end,
Unless the space team,
On mission '3.14'
Can wipe out the alien type Zend.

They have space lasers,
Which hopefully will save us.
They'll set them for kill,
We pray they won't get ill,
On space mission, '3.14'!

Matthew Tims (10)
St Bartholomew's CE Primary School, Haslemere

PLAYSTATION

My PlayStation can play.
It can shout.
My PlayStation can hiss.
It can hum.
My PlayStation can *roar.*
It's grey
Red
Blue
Black
It screams.
'What's that racket?'
'It's the PlayStation Dad!'
Ouch!
It gave me an electric shock.
It's puny, small, titchy and tiny.
Very dull in its colour.
Very, very amusing.
Vibration goes through you
Gets right to your back.
Game over!
Doh!

Robyn Lindsay (10)
Stoke Hill Primary School

HENRY

Henry is my best friend,
He can tidy my room,
Sucking up dirt,
Better than brooms.

Round and round,
Eating the dirt,
Running like mad,
Whoops! You've eaten my skirt.

Humming and singing,
Whirling and singing,
My room's nearly clean,
Henry is winning.

Kayleigh Meeks (10)
Stoke Hill Primary School

TELEVISION

I'm sitting down waiting,
For my machine to make it,
What will it look like?
Gigantic or small?
Smart or dull?
Will it play my
Favourite programme?
Will it make a video
Recorder down the bottom?
It's now hissing and roaring,
Will it be violent?
Don't know,
It's coming,
It's coming,
But it doesn't look anything,
Like I expected it to.

James Parker (11)
Stoke Hill Primary School

MACHINE

Grey, shiny, fun for all.
Small and very round, it makes me use it more and more.
It licks the silver disc as it goes in.
As it disappears into the dark night.
The lid slams, it makes a clatter.

It spins into action whirling and pumping.
The games start up, and are very entertaining.

Time flies past, and I play fast.
But game over.
The disc reappears from the dark depths of night.

Michael Pullen (11)
Stoke Hill Primary School

TRACTORS

Loud, angrily it thumps the ground
It stands alone
Whilst the sun shines brightly.
Like a monstrous scaly green dragon,
With its jaws snapping
The dark brown earth drips from its jaws
As it chews some more.
The monster purrs gently
As it trundles
On its way home.
Resting, readily for the next day.
Yet to come.

Billy Smith (10)
Stoke Hill Primary School

ROVER

It's big; it's not small
It's long; it's not tall
It roars at the oily ground
As it shoots by the old dog pound
Its eyes glow on the road
We nearly hit a juicy toad
It purrs very loud
As it looks at the cloud
Its eyes glow brightly
As the sky gets darker
The moonlit doors shine
As the car shoots past
It's racing green
It's a killing machine
It's loud
It's proud
It's roaring at the crowd
Growling and roaring
It's speeding it's leading
It's way too fast
Bigger than a blast
It whistles
It's bumping along
We are singing a song
Now we are here
It is time for a beer.

Tara Harris (10)
Stoke Hill Primary School

BOTTLE OPENER

It's black like a shell,
It's darker than hell,
It's blue like the sea,
It's just like you and me.

Its head's in a spin,
It flew in the bin,
Its arms are long and thin,
It just pulls in.

Into the cork burning,
Twisting and turning,
Heaving and weaving,
Kneeling and peeling.

Amy Purchese (11)
Stoke Hill Primary School

MY MACHINE

My machine is enormous and wide
It's light grey all over.
It's silent and noisy
It splutters when it prints.
It moves up and down
Around and around.
It plays music songs and raps
From pop stars all over the world.
It clickers and clackers
It's entertaining and exciting.
It pushes and pulls
It's got a head and a neck.
It's shiny and bright
Smooth and rough,
It's large and squared.
It's holey where the noise is
It clicks and clacks.
It makes me feel
Happy and sad
Funny and annoyed
It's pleasurable and enjoyable.

Gemma Burch (10)
Stoke Hill Primary School

CD PLAYER

Push the button
Up pops the tray
Insert the disk
Music will play

Around and around
Twisting and twirling
Clicking and clacking
The CD goes swirling

The machine is now pumping
Out shouts the songs
The speakers are thumping
All day long

My lovely knight in shining armour
Whoops! He chewed up my tape
Plays all day long never stops
Singing loudly, never makes a mistake.

Chelsea-Lee McWhinnie (11)
Stoke Hill Primary School

LIMOUSINE

Blue, green, purple its colour
Glistens in the sun.

It's lean, sleek and always gleaming.

Engine, purring, twisting and turning.

People turning their heads to see this
Limousine

As it glides down the busy street.

It nearly ran over people's feet

Twisting and turning,
Speeding and burning,
The wheels are turning on the
Limousine.

Leonie Webber (10)
Stoke Hill Primary School

LOG CUTTER

Smart and smooth
The cogs turn round
Smart and smooth
There is no sound

White and black
Are all the cogs
White and black
Turn all the logs

Left to right
Turn all the cogs
Left to right
Around the pogs

While turning
Are all the cogs
There were barks
Of lonesome dogs

As it stops
A lonesome cog
There are bells
Beware of fog

'We're all sound,'
All cogs shout
'But witches and wizards
Are out and about.'

As night falls
The lonesome cog
Gets slower and slower
Cutting the log

Hard work is over
All cogs sleep
All we hear now
Is God blessing sheep

Slow then fast
Up starts a cog
Slow then fast
Like an old hog

Slow then fast
A big fat cog
Slow then fast
On a steady jog

Hayleigh Harms (11)
Stoke Hill Primary School

MY MACHINE

My machine is enormous and wide and humungous.
It's light grey all over, all the cogs are
Spinning inside and going upside down.

It hums all the time and sometimes is quiet,
All the time it writes for me and does all my jobs.

It is entertaining when I play my games,
But it is annoying when I lose all.

It looks squared and smart
But it sometimes catches dust,
It's fun and makes me happy when I win.

It scans all my pictures so I can put them
On my wall, but when I have to go to bed
My bed flickers on my screen and
Looks like the stars.

In the morning I wake up early and I play
All my games and music,
When my music is loud it goes
Boom, boom, boom.

When it crashes it is silent, when it turns
Back on,
It makes me feel not lonely.

Amy Jacques (11)
Stoke Hill Primary School

THE OLD MAN

There was an old man who lived all alone
No one to talk to and no kind of home.
There's sometimes a shelter where he can go,
When he's desperate to get away from the rain and the snow.
His clothes are tatty and scrappy too
I feel so sorry, what shall I do?
At night I see him all alone
With the look in his eyes still munching on a bone,
I feel as if I want to give him a home.
What shall I do?
He's got a dog who walks the street at night
One little thing gives him a fright.
They're so scared of the big horrid world
They both lay down, their bodies curled.
Now it's night he's all out of sight
Where is he on this cold dark street?
I can hear the dog bark, its hard blistered feet
He's laying there weak; I let out a shriek!
He'll pass away slowly day after day.
'Goodnight and God bless.'

Shona-Leanne Fenton (10)
Stoke Hill Primary School

THE WINTER

In the winter.
I get freezing cold.
And when it snows.
The tree bark goes freezing cold.
The tree leaves fly away.
The hedgehogs start to hibernate.
While I'm indoors.
Sitting near the roasting hot fireplace.
Watching television.
I go outside and make a snow angel.
My sisters are having a snowball war.
Then we make a snowman.
As tall as my dad.
I run it over.
With my now gleaming bike.
We go in for dinner.

Patrick Ireland (10)
Stoke Hill Primary School

RAIN

Why does it always have to rain?
It's getting a bit of a pain!
When you go to school you have to wear wellies,
To walk across the waterlogged field.

The rain, why won't it go away?
It's drizzling down my window.
Every time it hits the ground it makes a pitter, patter sound,
I went downstairs and saw hailstones.

I went outside I heard a pitter patter,
I went outside with my wellies,
I was messing and splishing around in the puddles,
Then I heard a bud beam it was the orange sun, yippee!

In the sky I saw a rainbow,
Loud orange, sea blue and quiet violet,
Then I heard a loud drizzle!

In the sky I saw a black cloud,
In the sky I saw a blue drop,
In the road I saw a puddle,
In the road I saw a splash!

Taren Hewer (9)
Stoke Hill Primary School

WINTER

Always cold and wet,
Never warm and dry,
It always rains, never shines,
Trees lose their leaves,
Clouds everywhere,
Thunder and lightning,
Continuous rain,
Never any light,
Water God sends rain,
Summer's here
At last.

Raymond Harms (9)
Stoke Hill Primary School

A ROSE

I smell a rose.
Through my nose.
I love the smell.
It is the best.

A rose is deep red like blood.
With a prickly stem.
And it lives in a flowerbed.

Roses smell very nice.
They have the smell of sweet perfume.
Roses bring love and joy.
Mums like roses on Mother's Day.

Mark Hart (8)
Stoke Hill Primary School

SOMETIMES THE WEATHER

Sometimes the weather can be dim and dark.
Sometimes the clouds make rain all day.
Sometimes the weather can bring thunder all night.
Sometimes the weather could bring lightning both times!

Sometimes the wind can blow you over.
Sometimes the thunder can kill you from a tree.
Sometimes the snow is cold in the morning.
Sometimes there are hailstones coming at night!

Jay Burch (8)
Stoke Hill Primary School

MY BEST FRIEND

Do you know who my best friend is?
Could you guess?
She rolls around in the grass.
My best friend is my pup, Jess.

Do you know who my best friend is?
Don't you know?
She's fluffy and purrs all day long.
My best friend is my cat, Snow.

Do you know who my best friend is?
I'm sure you do.
She lives in a house and has a mouse.
My best friend is my next door neighbour.

Do you know who my best friend is?
I'm sure you do.
Look in the mirror
And you will see it's you.

Robert Vince (9)
Stoke Hill Primary School

THE SUNFLOWER

Me, you and the sunflower will always be there.
You can look in the sunflower and see me.
I can examine the sunflower and see you.
Me, you and the sunflower will always be there
I *love* sunflowers, so do you?
If you reach the sunflower, you can reach me.

Daniel Sommerville (10)
Stoke Hill Primary School

SCHOOL

School's good, school's bad,
And it is driving me really mad.
School's good, school's bad,
And harassing me really bad.

Work's good, work's bad,
And making my brain really mad,
School's good, school's bad,
School ends I'm really glad.

TV's good, TV's bad,
Making my eyes really bad,
TV's good, TV's bad,
Some even makes me sad.

Jamie Pankhurst (9)
Stoke Hill Primary School

FLOWERS

Flowers come out in the spring
They grow up to be thin
They collect their own water
They bring a spring feeling to your face
They smell like strawberries straight from the fields
Straight to your nose.

Michelle Taylor (10)
Stoke Hill Primary School

It's Spring, It's Spring

It's spring; it's spring -
When everyone sits round a roaring fire
Telling ghost stories!

It's spring; it's spring -
When everyone sneaks into everyone else's yard
And bashes up their snowman!

It's spring; it's spring -
When the last dead leaves fall from the trees
And granny falls off your toboggan.

It's spring; it's spring -
When you'd give your right arm
For a steaming hot bowl of soup!

It's spring; it's spring -
When you'd give your right leg
Not to be made to wash up after Christmas dinner!

It's spring; it's spring -
Isn't it?
It is very.

Lauren Horner (9)
Stoke Hill Primary School

THE SOGGY WEATHER

Up in the air the wind whistles,
Rapping at the windows
And rushing down the chimney, making eerie sounds
The wind has stopped and I'm out to play.

Trying to avoid the squishy grass
Jumping in the puddles as I pass
I've just got my friends wet
And they have gone in and I'm all alone
I am alone in the park.

I must go home straight away
Because their mums will tell me off
For the washing that I have to do
Oh no! One of them has knocked on the door
I'll pretend that I'm not in
And I will make myself a cheese sandwich.

The noise at the door is driving me up the wall
I can't hear the telly
They have gone away, hooray.

Arron Mills (9)
Stoke Hill Primary School

THE MOUSE

My new house has a little mouse,
Who lives behind the kitchen sink,
The only drink to drink,
Is my dad's Red Bull.
Now there's a whole family of mice,
They shall invade my mother's rice.
When I play Monopoly, when I role the dice,
The cheeky little mice they come and steal my dice.
I'm going to buy some head-lice
To put in their furry coats,
Hopefully I'll get my own back,
And hit them on the head,
Then they will be dead!
Ha ha!

Beckie Harvey (10)
Stoke Hill Primary School

THE GREEKS THAT ARE MAGIC

The gods and goddesses
So much to hear of them
So many stories of the Ancient Greeks
So many to enjoy.

So many stories of the famous ones
So many stories of Hercules
So many stories of the wicked Medusa.
So many stories of the high flying Perseus.

Weird clothes that the groovy Greeks wore
The groovy Greeks have funny houses
And funny weird names and funny schools
Weirder than ours.

The wicked Medusa
Who has ugly wicked eyes
Those wicked eyes that glow in the dark
Those wicked eyes that make people stiff as a rock.

And the amazing Hercules
The sword fighter
The murderer
The fearless one.

And the high flying Perseus
The one with the flying sandal
The one with the head of the stone killer Medusa.
The one with the mighty magic.

And Jason the man with the greatest name
The man with the greatest ship.
The man with the middy brain.

James Stevens (9)
Stoke Hill Primary School

SPACE

In space the sun shines so bright
On the planets called Pluto
Neptune, Venus
Saturn, Mercury
Earth, Uranus
Mars, Jupiter
Then there is the galaxy in a far away place
And if you face the sun it would sting your eyes
Also you would not be able to get near the sun
Because it is in a far distance.
The sun is so bright that you wouldn't like to touch it
The stars are bright but the star that is up first is the brightest star.
I think that Mars is a red planet and Neptune is the blue planet.

And I think Saturn is orange with a yellow ring.
I think Pluto is a bluish colour
I think that Mercury is a baking planet
Venus is the second roasting planet in space.

Paul Fenton (8)
Stoke Hill Primary School

BEACH

On the beach it is rocky.
People play in the sand.
They build castles
And go in the blue sea.

They like sunbathing.
When it is hot
They have lots of fun,
As they lay in the sun.

They play on rocks
And sit down on the sand.
They swim in the water,
And root in the sun!

Sabrina Fisher (9)
Stoke Hill Primary School

FOOTBALL

In football you have to punt a ball.
But make sure that you don't fall.
In football you try to score more goals.
But try not to lose.
In football you must tackle to score.
In football you are in two teams.
In football you will need a goalie if you don't want to lose.
We won the match today.

8 footballers on our team.
11 footballers on the other team.
Yesterday we lost the game.
But we're going to win tomorrow.
Today we scored 9 goals
But the other team scored 10 goals.
We lost again today.
We're going to win tomorrow.

Nathan Manley (9)
Stoke Hill Primary School

ME AND MY TED

As I go to bed,
I cuddle my Ted,
Sometimes I dream,
About what he would do
If he had a job.

If I have a nightmare,
I just squeeze him tight,
I can't sleep without him,
I see him as real
Pink Ted.

Rosanna Caffrey (9)
Stoughton Grange Junior School

SCHOOL

I like school
I think it's really cool.
I have one friend,
But he drives me round the bend.
My favourite subject is art,
Because I'm kind of smart.
But most of all,
I like school.

Darren Summerfield (10)
Stoughton Grange Junior School

FOOD

Some food is horrible,
Some food is delicious,
Some foods are in the middle.
Sometimes I fiddle
With my food.

My favourite is ice cream
It will whisk me off into a dream
Mash potatoes and fish
I like in my dish.

Sometimes I have a food fight
Then the sun shines bright
And after that there is a mess
All over the wall
It's slippery so I fall.

Zoe Phipps (10)
Stoughton Grange Junior School

ME AND MY RABBIT

All comfy in my bed
The adventures start to explode
First we're at the seaside
But soon the pirates come

Sometimes we're in the North Pole
We see penguins and polar bears
Big and small, cute and ugly,
Fierce and friendly
But we like them all

Then, the rain starts
I'm back in my bed
Warm and cosy
Just me . . . and my ted.

Emma Unwin (10)
Stoughton Grange Junior School

CHINA DOLLS

I feel so scared
I feel so frightened
Whenever I look at my china dolls
With their big eyes
That look at me
They just stare all day.
When I wake up I feel a creepy touch
Whenever I move they're still
Looking and looking at me.
Sometimes I wish to lock them up
But they're still sitting and staring
At me with their long hair and their
Pale faces and their black dresses.
Sometimes in my dreams
They all come after me
I can't go on anymore.

Natasha Etherington (10)
Stoughton Grange Junior School

AT THE WOODS

Have you ever seen the water
When it's glistening in the moonlight?
Seeing your reflection
Listening to the owls
Hooting as they watch
The little birds sleep.

You can almost see the trees
Walking as they sway.

The woods are like my home
I know them so well.

Emma White (10)
Stoughton Grange Junior School

MY RABBIT

My rabbit is so furry.
I can take her in and play with her.
She is so beautiful and cuddly.
Her tail is a furry ball.
She has wonderful eyes.
Her eyes are like a staring ball.

Damien Hann (9)
Stoughton Grange Junior School

SOMEWHERE IN OUR SCHOOL TODAY

360 ravenous children are goggling at the clock eager for lunch.
A teacher is chuckling merrily at a piece of work writing comments.
Two petrified boys are waiting for the head teacher to tell them off.
Three energetic girls are typing veraciously at a computer
Flicking through books packed with information.
A maths teacher is encouraging her pupil, desperate he gets it correct.
360 children scramble out of school set to gaze at the TV
While stuffing their faces with food.

Angharad Norris (10)
Worplesdon Primary School

SOMEWHERE IN OUR SCHOOL TODAY

A team of fifteen mud splattered rugby players
Are enthusiastically playing a game of rugby.
The seven infants noisily banging on the bass drum
As their teacher is telling them off.
A group of budding scientists
Are learning about how the moon travels around the world.
Over 200 boys are playing in the biggest match of the year.
Twenty seven poetic authors are writing a story.

Matthew Smith (9)
Worplesdon Primary School

SOMEWHERE IN OUR SCHOOL TODAY . . .

A bunch of juniors are happily dancing about to some cheerful music.
A few nervous narrators are forgetting their lines as they
Try to tell the story of 'Little Monsters'.
A class of fidgeting infants are trying to read 'The Magic Key'
To their teacher, with great difficulty.
A few musicians are vigorously clashing at the cymbals,
Trying to produce the latest pop music.
Twenty brilliant netball players are anxiously trying
To keep the ball away from the other team.

Rosie Sandell (10)
Worplesdon Primary School

SOMEWHERE IN OUR SCHOOL TODAY

Thirty-three clever poets are writing a mysterious poem on
Goosebumps.
Five musicians are playing frantically on the bongos in music.
Eight budding divers are splashing in the pool before
Doing the butterfly, in record time.
Fourteen brilliant basketball players are anxiously
Trying to get a hoop, to win the game in PE.
Twenty-nine children are licking their lips as they are
About to taste home-made bread in cooking.
Nine artists are getting excited because they are
About to try and draw a Monet picture.

Rhiannon Jones (10)
Worplesdon Primary School

SOMEWHERE IN OUR SCHOOL TODAY . . .

Thirty energetic athletes are vigorously shooting
Like bullets up the racetrack.

A hall full of bored children are gazing longingly out of the
Window hoping that assembly will end soon.

Twenty-seven eager children are scrabbling frantically to get to break.

A shoal of white-faced swimmers are noisily splashing in an icy pool.

A bunch of hungry children are staring hopefully at the clock
As the second hand slowly makes its way to half-past, lunchtime.

A crocodile of happy children are madly tearing out of school.

Kate Robarts (9)
Worplesdon Primary School

SOMEWHERE IN OUR SCHOOL TODAY . . .

Nine children are writing a magnificent story.
Five infants are being told off for using the wrong programme
                                        on the computer.
A handful of children are eating their lunch.
Seven pupils are talking about the latest games for the PlayStation.
A couple are surfing the web for science information.

Marcus Butcher (10)
Worplesdon Primary School

SOMEWHERE IN OUR SCHOOL TODAY . . .

A strict year one teacher is firmly marching her class down
The corridor, into assembly.

Twenty-four giggling juniors are randomly scanning
The smooth and shiny pages of a human body book.

A trembling infant is nervously waiting for his meningitis jab,
His face already white with fear.

Twenty-eight half-asleep year fours are dully listening to their
boring teacher
Who's droning on about the life cycle of a beetroot.

A mud-covered Year 6 is frantically charging towards
The touchdown line, his head like a battering ram.

Matthew Parsons (10)
Worplesdon Primary School

SOMEWHERE IN OUR SCHOOL TODAY

A pair of cheeky boys are being shouted at by the headmaster,
A tinkerous toddler, waiting for his brother to come out of school,
Is weeping sadly having stumbled on the cobbled paving,
A crowd of shy, giggling girls are scanning
A torn up old map of the USSR,
A group of enthusiastic boys are vigorously spinning
A cracked globe trying to track the journey of Sir Francis Drake
And a frustrated Year six is yanking her hair out as the grinning teacher
Calls out mind-boggling algebra questions.

Max Makin (10)
Worplesdon Primary School

SOMEWHERE IN OUR SCHOOL TODAY . . .

Twenty-eight brainy children frantically flicking through the pages
Of a human body book, trying to find more information
Twenty-nine children are puffing and panting after running
Around the playground twice trying to warm up.
Thirty-three children are hitting drums with all their might.
One hundred children are dancing the night away at the disco.
Thirty manic children are running around playing 'It'.

Stephen Cox (9)
Worplesdon Primary School

SOMEWHERE IN OUR SCHOOL TODAY

The over-excited students of Worplesdon School
Are staring at a very exciting and humorous
Class assembly just before break,
The excited children of Jays are staring at the computer
Watching the teacher show us how to do a power point presentation,
The annoyed sportsmen are trying their hardest
To climb up a rope to get to the top,
The mathematicians of Jays are rushing
Through their maths sheets to finish,
The children are vigorously scribbling in their books
Trying not to make a mistake.

Richard Woods (10)
Worplesdon Primary School

SOMEWHERE IN OUR SCHOOL TODAY . . .

The mysterious clever teachers are mumbling
All day long about the treacherous children.
Thirty-two cheeky footballers are sprinting with the disgusting ball
Hoping to score a goal.
Two extremely clever poets are thinking carefully
About their rhyming letters.
Twenty bored children are ignoring what the teachers say about RE.
Five excited children are setting up a highly dangerous experiment
In the dark room.

Matthew Farminer (10)
Worplesdon Primary School

SOMEWHERE IN OUR SCHOOL TODAY . . .

Thirty starving children are queuing, stomachs rumbling,
Annoying each other enormously.
Thirty-five expert footballers are planning how to cunningly
         win the cup.
Twenty-six unenthusiastic historians are starting a battle of Hastings
         themselves,
Lobbing inky pens and sharp pencils in all directions.
A class of highly interested musicians are banging like thunder
On their drums, driving their teacher up the wall,
However hard they try not to.
A class of keen travellers are doing geography,
Mistaking Mongolia for Australia.

James Caven (9)
Worplesdon Primary School

SOMEWHERE IN OUR SCHOOL TODAY . . .

30 excited authors are writing strange stories.
A bunch of eager artists covered in paint are painting a water picture.
Some wild musicians are banging loudly
On the school's massive bass drum.
A class full of scientists are carefully trying out an experiment.
Bunches of mathematicians are carefully trying out difficult fractions.
A team full of netball players are speeding around the court
Trying to win.

Anna Baker (10)
Worplesdon Primary School

SOMEWHERE IN OUR SCHOOL TODAY . . .

A class of badly behaved musicians are vigorously banging
On drums while the teacher is bellowing at them.
A bunch of 26 noisy, giggling writers are brainstorming
A mystery problem for their cliffhanging stories.
A class of inquisitive children are noisily flicking
Through history books to find exciting facts about historic buildings.
A group of enthusiastic children are rapidly shouting out answers
As the teacher is writing questions on the board.
2 mischievous boys are quivering as the head teacher
Bellows down at their guilty faces.

Hannah Luxford (9)
Worplesdon Primary School

SOMEWHERE IN OUR SCHOOL TODAY ...

A class shivering in the swimming pool are trying to keep warm.
Noisy boys are banging on drums while getting shouted at.
29 messy artists are concentrating as they stare at their
horrible drawings.
1 nervous infant is staring at a needle as the nurse pokes him in his arm.
Quiet scientists are quietly making up experiments.

Amy Hirst (9)
Worplesdon Primary School